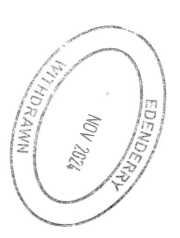

ANTIBIOTICS

By Joanna Brundle

BookLife
PUBLISHING

©2019
BookLife Publishing Ltd.
King's Lynn
Norfolk PE30 4LS

All rights reserved.
Printed in Malaysia.

A catalogue record for this book is
available from the British Library.

ISBN: 978-1-78637-539-1

Written by:
Joanna Brundle

Edited by:
Kirsty Holmes

Designed by:
Dan Scase

All facts, statistics, web addresses
and URLs in this book were verified
as valid and accurate at time of
writing. No responsibility for any
changes to external websites or
references can be accepted by
either the author or publisher.

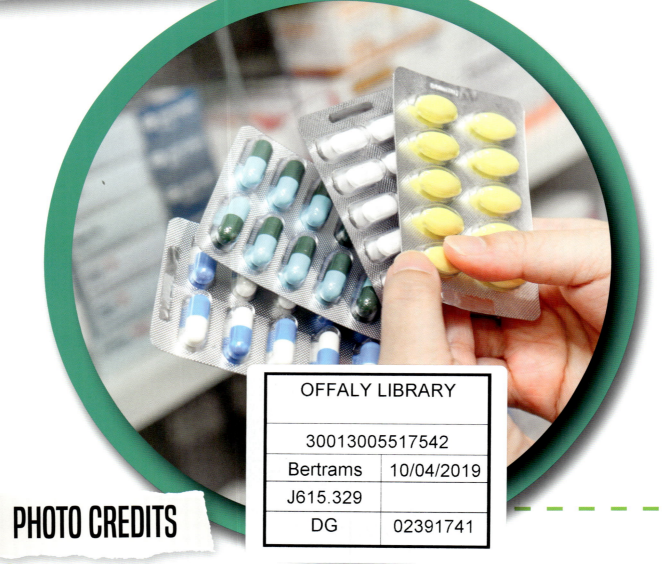

PHOTO CREDITS

Front Cover – Leone_V, Dragon Images, BLACKDAY, Oxy_gen, StudioAz, vector toon. 2 – i viewfinder. 3 – AVA Bitter. 4 – Tyler Olson, Ilike. 5 – Marzolino, nokwalai. 6 – Sebastian Kaulitzki, Kateryna Kon. 7 – Kateryna Kon, Adul10, Flas100. 8&9 – Macrovector. 10 – Pattikky, Satirus, WhiteDragon. 11 – chrisdorney, Awe Inspiring Images, Imperial War Museums. 12 – Janusz Pienkowski, angellodeco, Eric Isselee. 13 – Crulina 98, margouillat photo, wu hsiung. 14 – breakermaximus. 15 – Kateryna Kon, Syda Productions, GoldVectorLine. 16 – ElRoi, Andrey_Popov. 17 – Kateryna Kon. 18&19 – jijomathaidesigners, MBLifestyle, sittichai nilsree, Casa nayafana, wavebreakmedia, David Tadevosian. 20 – margouillat photo, Phawat, AVA Bitter. 21 – Kateryna Kon. 22 – Andrei_M, Titov Nikolai. 23 – 18percentgrey. 24 – krumanop, Maksim M. 25 – Chansom Pantip, B Calkins. 26 – Dan Race, RGtimeline, Nadia Buravleva. 27 – Valery121283, Design_Cells. 28 – Everett Historical, Tony Baggett. 29 – g215, Liga Cerina, Rigamondis. 30 – Natural Mosart, Heike Rau, Frank Bach. Borders on all pages – Leone_V. Antibiotic vectors throughout – Oxy_gen. Ripped paper throughout – BLACKDAY. Heart rate vector – StudioAz. Logo heart – vector toon. Images are courtesy of Shutterstock.com. With thanks to Getty Images, Thinkstock Photo and iStockphoto.

LIFE-SAVING SCIENCE

Words that look like THIS can be found in the glossary on page 31.

Some words used in this book have different singular and plural forms. Use this table to help you.

SINGULAR	SAY:	PLURAL	SAY:
Bacterium	Back-TEER-ee-um	Bacteria	Back-TEER-ee-ah
Staphylococcus	Staf-i-low-COC-us	Staphylococci	Staf-i-low-COC-eye
Streptococcus	Strep-toe-COC-us	Streptococci	Strep-to-COC-eye

THE WORLD OF MEDICINE

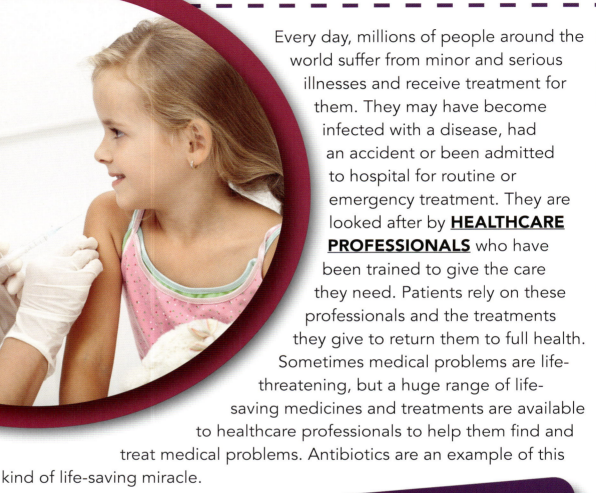

Every day, millions of people around the world suffer from minor and serious illnesses and receive treatment for them. They may have become infected with a disease, had an accident or been admitted to hospital for routine or emergency treatment. They are looked after by **HEALTHCARE PROFESSIONALS** who have been trained to give the care they need. Patients rely on these professionals and the treatments they give to return them to full health. Sometimes medical problems are life-threatening, but a huge range of life-saving medicines and treatments are available to healthcare professionals to help them find and treat medical problems. Antibiotics are an example of this kind of life-saving miracle.

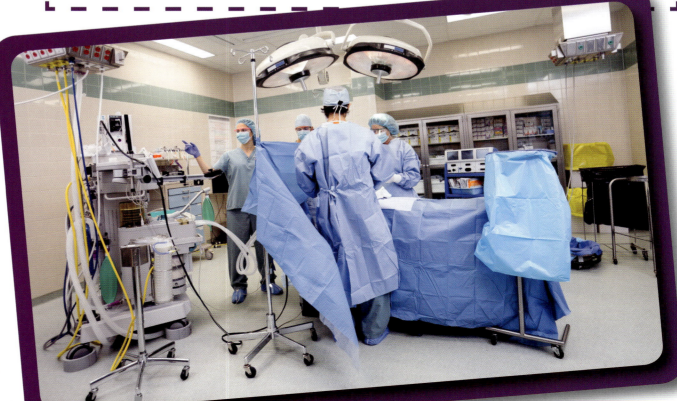

Since 1900, worldwide average life expectancy (the amount of time that a newborn baby is expected to live for) has more than doubled and is now over 70 years. Scientists are predicting that average life expectancy will eventually reach over 100 years in some societies. There are many reasons for this. Improved healthcare, particularly a better understanding of the causes and treatment of infections, has been very important. In many parts of the world, good health and healthcare are now accepted as normal parts of life, so it is easy to forget that this has not always been the case, and still isn't in some places. In the past, even minor cuts and grazes could cause life-threatening infections. Many women died from infections after childbirth. Diseases such as **PNEUMONIA** (say: new-MOAN-EE-ah) and **TUBERCULOSIS** (say: tu-BER-cu-low-sis), which are now easily treated, were often deadly. In this book, we shall be taking a look at the life-saving role of antibiotics.

In Victorian times, illnesses such as **WHOOPING COUGH** (say: hooping coff), pneumonia, tuberculosis and **SCARLET FEVER** caused thousands of deaths.

FACT

THE ANCIENT EGYPTIANS USED PLANTS, SUCH AS GARLIC, TO TREAT INFECTIONS BUT BELIEVED THAT ILLNESSES WERE CAUSED BY EVIL SPIRITS.

WHAT ARE ANTIBIOTICS?

ILLUSTRATION OF PHAGOCYTE ENGULFING A BACTERIUM

The human body is constantly in contact with pathogens. Pathogens are **MICROSCOPIC** organisms, such as **BACTERIA**, that can cause disease if they enter the bloodstream or body tissues. These harmful bacteria are often called 'germs'. They are found everywhere: in water, food, soil, and in the air, and on surfaces such as doors and tables.

ILLUSTRATION OF A LYMPHOCYTE

Every part of the human body, from the ears and eyes to the digestive system, is equipped to provide a barrier against infection. Pathogens that do manage to enter the body are dealt with by two types of a cell found in blood, called white blood cells. Phagocytes (say: FAY-guh-sites) engulf and destroy pathogens. Lymphocytes (say: LIM-fuh-sites) recognise substances found on the surface of pathogens, called antigens. They then make antibodies, which are substances that stick to the pathogens and mark them out for attack. Lymphocytes also produce substances called antitoxins. These **NEUTRALISE** poisonous substances called toxins that are released by some harmful bacteria.

Sometimes, harmful bacteria grow and multiply very quickly, despite the body's defences. The human body provides excellent conditions for bacteria to multiply – warmth, nutrients and moisture. Each bacterium can split into two new bacteria roughly every 20 minutes; so after just an hour, a single bacterium can become eight bacteria. If harmful bacteria multiply out of control, the body needs extra help to fight the infection. Antibiotics are used for this purpose. They are medicines that either kill the harmful bacteria or stop them from multiplying.

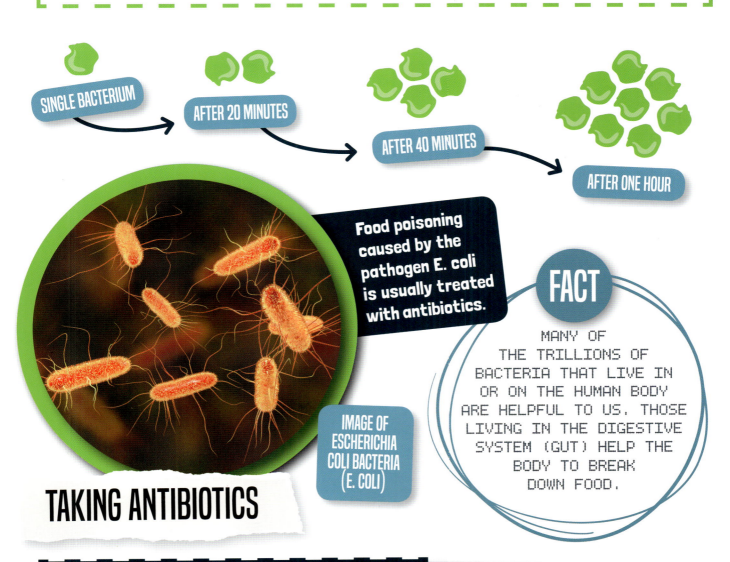

SINGLE BACTERIUM

AFTER 20 MINUTES

AFTER 40 MINUTES

AFTER ONE HOUR

Food poisoning caused by the pathogen E. coli is usually treated with antibiotics.

FACT

MANY OF THE TRILLIONS OF BACTERIA THAT LIVE IN OR ON THE HUMAN BODY ARE HELPFUL TO US. THOSE LIVING IN THE DIGESTIVE SYSTEM (GUT) HELP THE BODY TO BREAK DOWN FOOD.

IMAGE OF ESCHERICHIA COLI BACTERIA (E. COLI)

TAKING ANTIBIOTICS

Antibiotics are usually prescribed by a doctor or specialist nurse and are issued at a **PHARMACY**. Antibiotics can be swallowed as tablets or liquids. Topical antibiotics are creams, drops or sprays that are applied directly to an infected area, for example to treat a skin infection. Serious infections are often treated in hospitals by an injection or drip, directly into the bloodstream.

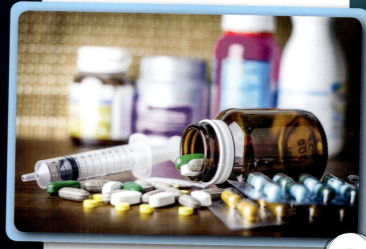

NATURAL DEFENCES AGAINST INFECTION

As well as the white blood cells that make up part of the **IMMUNE SYSTEM**, the human body has many ways of defending itself from invading bacteria. Antibiotics are only needed if these defences fail and if bacteria then multiply out of control.

Many foods may contain harmful bacteria that can cause food poisoning. These include: unwashed fruit and vegetables, raw meat and fish, **UNPASTEURISED** milk or cheese, and eggs. Washing and cooking food properly reduces the risk. Most of the harmful bacteria in the food we eat is killed by a substance called hydrochloric acid, found in our stomachs. The acid does us no harm but is strong enough to kill off bacteria.

Our skin acts as a natural barrier against pathogens. If we cut ourselves, blood rushes to the wound and **PLATELETS** help the red blood cells to form a clot. White blood cells engulf any bacteria that enter (see page 6). The clot and the scab (which forms later) protect the wound from infection. Organs in the skin, called sebaceous glands, produce an oily substance called sebum. Sebum contains substances that break down the cell wall – or outer layer – of harmful bacteria.

The fluid that covers our eyes contains lysozymes – substances that destroy bacteria by breaking down their cell walls. Lysozymes are also found in saliva, breast milk and **MUCUS**.

The nose and airways are lined with sticky mucus and tiny hairs called cilia (say: silly-uh). These help to trap bacteria carried in the air and prevent them from reaching the lungs. Sneezing or blowing the nose gets rid of bacteria trapped in mucus. Hairs in the trachea (the pipe that runs from the nose to the lungs) waft mucus and trapped pathogens up to the throat. They are then coughed out or swallowed into the stomach.

The lymphatic system is a network that spreads throughout the body. As well as draining a fluid called lymph from the body, it also stores lymphocytes (see page 6) and filters out harmful bacteria. The spleen also does these jobs.

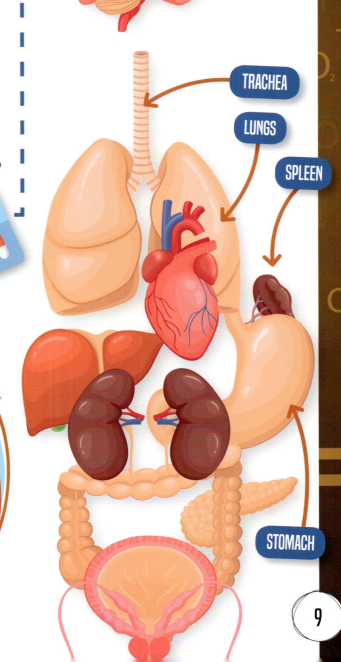

TRACHEA

LUNGS

SPLEEN

STOMACH

FACT

THE BODY'S IMMUNE SYSTEM CAN REACT BADLY TO SUBSTANCES THAT ARE HARMLESS TO MOST PEOPLE. THIS IS CALLED AN ALLERGIC REACTION. SOME PEOPLE ARE ALLERGIC TO SOME ANTIBIOTICS AND A SERIOUS REACTION CAN BE FATAL.

THE DISCOVERY OF ANTIBIOTICS

COLONIES OF PENICILLIUM MOULD

The first antibiotic, penicillin, was discovered by accident by Alexander Fleming, a Scottish **MICROBIOLOGIST** and doctor. Fleming, who was well-known for having an untidy **LABORATORY**, had been investigating a bacterium called Staphylococcus aureus. In August 1928, he left his laboratory at St Mary's Hospital in London, to go on holiday, leaving several **PETRI DISHES** stacked up on a counter – he was famously messy, and did not wash the dishes before going away. They contained cultures – or growths – of the bacteria. On his return, on the 3rd of September 1928, Fleming noticed that a culture of the bacteria that he had left out had become contaminated with a mould. This mould was later identified as Penicillium notatum. Looking more closely, Fleming then noticed that colonies of Staphylococci that were next to the mould had been destroyed. He had, by pure chance, made a discovery that was to prove a turning point in medicine – a substance that killed off bacteria. Fleming called the antibiotic 'mould juice', but later renamed it penicillin, after the mould that had produced it.

FACT

IN THE 1880S, GERMAN DOCTORS OSCAR LOWE AND RUDOLPH EMMERICH HAD DEVELOPED AN EARLY FORM OF ANTIBIOTIC. ALTHOUGH EFFECTIVE FOR SOME PATIENTS, IT PROVED TO BE POISONOUS, KILLING OTHERS, SO ITS USE WAS STOPPED.

CULTURE OF STAPHYLOCOCCUS AUREUS

It took Fleming several weeks to produce enough of the mould to be certain of his discovery. He is famously quoted as saying: "When I woke up… on 28 September 1928, I certainly didn't plan to revolutionise all medicine by discovering the world's first antibiotic, or bacteria killer. But I guess that's exactly what I did."

SIR ALEXANDER FLEMING 1881-1955 DISCOVERED PENICILLIN IN THE SECOND STOREY ROOM ABOVE THIS PLAQUE

Fleming carried out further **RESEARCH** and was able to show that penicillin was effective against a range of bacteria. He published his work, presenting it to the Medical Research Club – a group of scientists and doctors – in London in February, 1928. But nobody in the medical world was interested and the possible use of his discovery in fighting infection was ignored. Fleming decided to move on to another area of study.

FLOREY, CHAIN AND HEATLEY

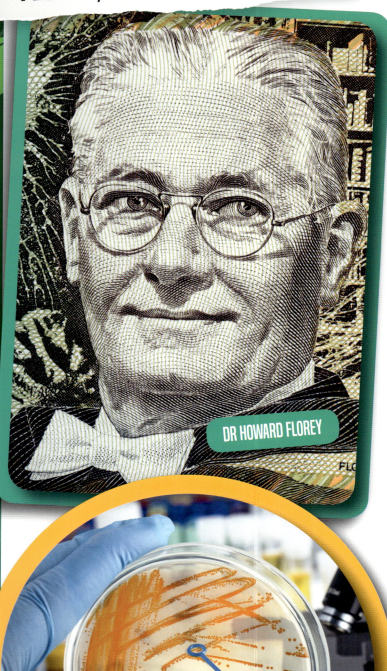

DR HOWARD FLOREY

COLONIES OF STREPTOCOCCI

In 1938, Dr Howard Florey, a **PROFESSOR** at the University of Oxford, found Fleming's research on the Penicillium mould. He decided to investigate and to develop penicillin further. Together with his colleagues, Ernst Chain and Norman Heatley, he began the process. Heatley was responsible for growing enough of the mould for experiments to be carried out. The team needed to isolate the active substance that was causing the antibiotic effect. By March 1940, they were able to begin experiments on mice. They infected the mice with a deadly bacterium, Streptococcus. Half the mice received penicillin injections and survived. The other half didn't have injections and died. Florey realised he could now begin testing the antibiotic on humans. The problem was how to produce enough of it – it would take 2,000 litres of 'mould juice' to produce the pure penicillin needed to treat just one person.

The mice that were given penicillin survived. This was an important step forward.

Heatley used every available container he could find to grow the penicillin mould and then remove the 'mould juice'. He went to a biscuit factory in the nearby town of Reading, where he was given biscuit tins to use. He even used bedpans given by the nearby John Radcliffe Hospital in Oxford! But it still was not enough. In 1941, Florey and Heatley travelled to the US, where they worked with American scientists and **DRUG COMPANIES** to try to solve the problem. Mary Hunt, a laboratory assistant, noticed that a cantaloupe melon she had found at a market had a golden mould growing on it. This mould was Penicillium chrysogenum (say: cry-so-JEN-um). It produced much more penicillin than Fleming's species produced. It was an important step forward which, like Fleming's original discovery, had happened by chance.

PENICILLIUM CHRYSOGENUM

13

Further developments, including the use of X-rays, eventually ensured that by 1944, tens of thousands of people were being successfully treated for infections using antibiotics. Things had moved very quickly since the first human trial of penicillin. A patient in the John Radcliffe Hospital, Police Constable Albert Alexander, had sustained a cut to his face in September 1940, either from a bombing raid or from a rose bush – details of the story vary. One eye became infected and was removed and the infection then spread to his shoulder and lungs. He was given a series of penicillin injections in February 1941 and began a miraculous recovery – until the available penicillin ran out. He died a few weeks later. The antibiotic power of penicillin was obvious, but it was also clear that it was essential to have enough available to treat a patient until the infection had completely disappeared.

FACT

IN 1945, FLEMING, FLOREY AND CHAIN SHARED THE **NOBEL PRIZE** IN MEDICINE FOR THEIR ROLES IN DISCOVERING AND PRODUCING THE FIRST WIDELY AVAILABLE ANTIBIOTIC.

Penicillin went into mass production during the later stages of World War II. Thousands of soldiers, who would otherwise have died from their injuries, were successfully treated.

Tuberculosis is estimated to have killed one billion people worldwide in the last two centuries.

The widespread introduction of penicillin was the start of what is sometimes called the golden age of antibiotic discovery. Most of the classes of antibiotics that we use today were discovered in the 1940s and 1950s. In 1943, a team of scientists in the US, led by Selman Waksman, discovered an antibiotic produced by a bacterium found in soil: Streptomyces griseus (say: strep-TOE-my-sees gree-see-us). This antibiotic, which was named streptomycin, was the first to be effective in treating tuberculosis. In an effort to discover more new classes of antibiotics, scientists began analysing soil samples from all around the world, even encouraging religious **MISSIONARIES** in remote places to collect samples. In 1953, a new antibiotic, vancomycin, was discovered in a soil sample from Borneo. Between 1940 and 1962, over 20 new classes of antibiotics became available, but the discovery of new classes slowed down in the late 1960s. A new class of antibiotic, called teixobactin, that is produced by a bacterium found in soil, was discovered in 2015, but it is still being tested before trials on humans can begin.

Thorough checks and tests, called clinical trials, have to be carried out on new medicines before they can be licensed to treat humans.

HOW DO ANTIBIOTICS WORK?

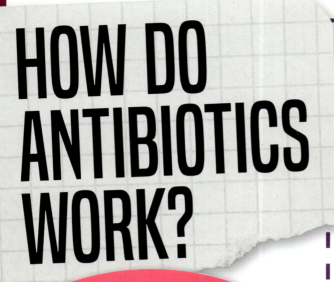

Different types of antibiotic work in different ways. Bactericidal antibiotics work by killing off the bacteria causing an infection. Cells are the tiny building blocks that make up all living organisms. The cell wall is the outer layer that encloses and gives support to some types of bacterial cell. Bacteria build this cell wall by joining **MOLECULES** together. Bactericidal antibiotics work by blocking the building of the cell wall. Without the support of the cell wall, the cell collapses and its contents leak out. Penicillin is an example of this type of antibiotic, which are called beta-lactam antibiotics.

Have you ever had a bacterial throat infection like this? You may have been treated with a bactericidal antibiotic such as penicillin.

Ear infections in children are often treated with a macrolide called erithromycin.

Left untreated, harmful bacteria within the body can grow and multiply rapidly. Bacteriostatic antibiotics work by preventing this from happening. Some bacteriostatic antibiotics, called macrolides, work by stopping bacterial cells from building **PROTEINS** that they need to survive. Others, called quinolones (say: QUIN-uh-lones), work by damaging a cell's **DNA**. DNA is the material that carries information about how development takes place.

FACT

DNA STANDS FOR DEOXYRIBONUCLEIC (SAY: DEE-OX-EE-RYE-BO-NEW-CLAY-ICK) ACID.

Are you now wondering how antibiotics are able to attack bacterial cells without damaging other cells in our bodies? It's a very good question! They are able to do this because, although bacterial cells and human cells are similar in some ways, they are very different in others. Human cells, for example, do not have a cell wall. They also have different ways of making proteins and DNA that mean antibiotics do not damage them.

NARROW- AND BROAD-SPECTRUM ANTIBIOTICS

Gram-positive bacteria are bacterial cells that have a thick, loose outer wall that allows many types of antibiotic to pass through. Gram-negative bacteria have a cell covering that is thin, but difficult to pass through, rather like a bullet-proof vest. The range of bacteria that an antibiotic attacks is called its 'spectrum of action'. Broad-spectrum antibiotics kill or prevent the growth of a wide range of infection-causing bacteria, including gram-positive and gram-negative. Narrow-spectrum antibiotics (sometimes called limited-spectrum antibiotics) are only effective against a particular organism. They are used when the particular bacterium causing an infection is known.

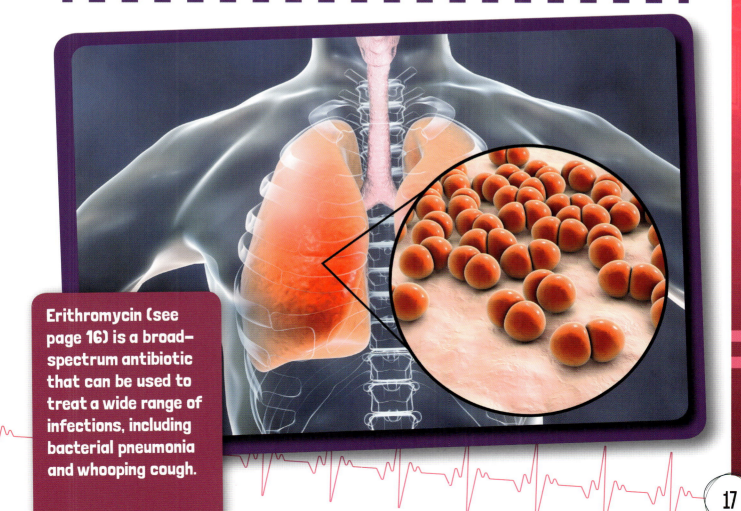

Erithromycin (see page 16) is a broad-spectrum antibiotic that can be used to treat a wide range of infections, including bacterial pneumonia and whooping cough.

USES OF ANTIBIOTICS

Before treating a patient for an infection, a doctor needs to decide if the infection is caused by bacteria or by a **VIRUS**. Antibiotics are only effective against bacterial infections. They are not effective against viruses, which may require treatment with different drugs called antivirals.

Viruses cause illnesses like the common cold and flu.

Antibiotics are used to treat common infections, such as **BRONCHITIS**, conjunctivitis and bacterial throat and ear infections.

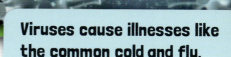
IMPETIGO

Conjunctivitis causes sore, red eyes and is usually treated with antibiotic drops.

Antibiotics are used to treat infections that could spread easily to other people, such as the skin disease impetigo.

Antibiotics are used to treat illnesses that can cause serious complications. Cellulitis, for example, can spread to other parts of the body, including the blood and bones.

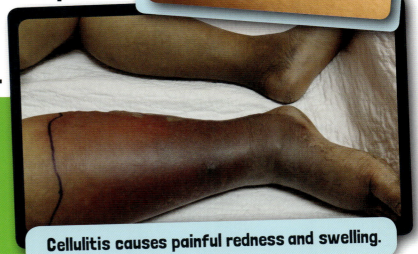
Cellulitis causes painful redness and swelling.

Sometimes, antibiotics are used to prevent infection, rather than to treat it. This type of treatment, called prophylaxis (say: prof-ih-lax-sis), is often used before operations on parts of the body with a high risk of infection, for example the **BOWEL**. Antibiotics are also used to prevent infection in people whose immune system is weak, for example **HIV** patients.

Dentists prescribe antibiotics for infections in the mouth, for example infection of the glands that produce saliva or infection following the removal of a tooth.

The success of all operations, including heart, kidney and lung transplants, heart surgery and replacement of knee and hip joints, depends on antibiotics to prevent infection after surgery.

In wars throughout history, infection has caused more deaths than injuries in battle. As we read on page 14, the widespread introduction of penicillin in 1944 meant that in World War II, death rates from infection reduced dramatically and fewer soldiers had to have infected limbs amputated. At this time, penicillin became known as 'the wonder drug'.

Antibiotics are used to treat **LIVESTOCK** either for existing infection or to prevent infection. A single animal may be treated, or a group of animals if one is infected. Antibiotics are also used to make animals grow faster and bigger but use for this purpose is reducing.

Animals that live very close to one another, such as these chickens that are kept indoors, are often given antibiotics to prevent infection.

USING ANTIBIOTICS SAFELY

The best way to avoid having to use antibiotics at all is to keep your immune system healthy. You can help to do this by eating a healthy diet that includes fruit, vegetables, nuts and seeds, by getting enough sleep and by doing plenty of exercise.

If you do need to take antibiotics, make sure that you take the amount prescribed by the doctor. Take them regularly and always finish the course, even if you feel better, otherwise the infection may return. Most antibiotics should be stored at room temperature in dry conditions but some need to be kept in the fridge, so always check. Some need to be taken on an empty stomach whereas others should be taken after you have eaten.

Antibiotics for children are often given as liquid medicine that is easier to swallow than a tablet.

SIDE EFFECTS OF ANTIBIOTICS

Antibiotics can cause side effects – unwanted effects that happen in addition to the intended effect of curing infection. The side effects of antibiotics can include nausea, vomiting, stomach pain, rashes and headaches. Not everyone suffers side effects. Around one person in fifteen is allergic to some antibiotics, especially penicillin. A serious allergic reaction can be fatal so always tell a doctor if you are allergic to penicillin.

GOOD BACTERIA

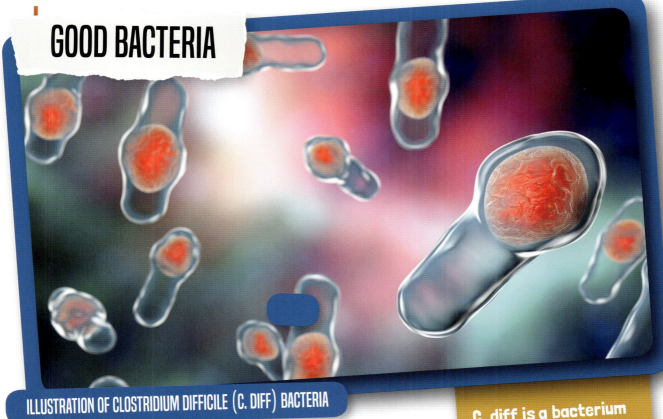

ILLUSTRATION OF CLOSTRIDIUM DIFFICILE (C. DIFF) BACTERIA

C. diff is a bacterium that can infect the digestive system of people whose good gut bacteria have been damaged by taking antibiotics, especially in hospitals and care homes.

The human body is home to trillions of helpful bacteria. These bacteria help to digest food, build the immune system and protect against infection caused by harmful bacteria. Whilst antibiotics deal effectively with harmful bacteria, they also kill off good bacteria that we need to stay healthy. This can upset the delicate balance of bacteria in the gut, causing diarrhoea (say: die-uh-ree-ah). After taking antibiotics, some people need help to return to this balance and may take probiotics. Probiotics are live bacteria and yeasts, found in some foods, such as live yoghurts, or taken as tablets. Some healthcare professionals question whether probiotics are effective.

THE RISE OF RESISTANCE

Just like humans, bacteria contain DNA, which can mutate – or change – just as it does in humans. When humans take antibiotics to treat a bacterial infection, most of the bacteria are killed off. However, in some cases, the bacteria mutate so that the antibiotics cannot kill them.

The mutant bacteria that survive quickly multiply, forming a new population of bacteria that cannot be killed by – or are resistant to – the antibiotic used. This is antibiotic resistance, which is becoming an increasingly serious threat to people all around the world. Antibiotic-resistant bacteria are found in people, animals, food and the environment and can spread easily from person to person, and between people and animals. An animal or human that has been given antibiotics even just once in their lifetime may contain mutant antibiotic-resistant bacteria.

FACT

BACTERIA THAT DEVELOP RESISTANCE TO ANTIBIOTICS ARE OFTEN CALLED SUPERBUGS.

1

DIVIDING BACTERIA

2

During division, a bacterium mutates, making it resistant to the antibiotic being used.

3

Most bacteria are killed by the antibiotic, but the antibiotic-resistant bacterium is unaffected.

4

Resistant bacteria multiply, forming a new population of bacteria that cannot be treated with the original antibiotic.

WHY IS ANTIBIOTIC RESISTANCE INCREASING?

The more humans that use antibiotics, the more chances we give bacteria to develop resistance. The less we use them, the fewer opportunities bacteria have to develop and share resistance. The effectiveness of antibiotics has, in one sense, been part of the problem. People have come to rely on them so much that they have taken them too often, either for infections that would have cleared up on their own or for viral infections which cannot be cured with antibiotics. Patients often do not finish their course of antibiotics, stopping early because they feel better. This can lead to reinfection that is harder to treat because the infection-causing bacteria have developed resistance. Many people have been given antibiotics at a very young age and have taken many courses of them throughout their lives. Doctors have been partly to blame for giving prescriptions for antibiotics that were not necessary.

FACT

IT HAS BEEN ESTIMATED THAT AS MUCH AS 30% OF ALL ANTIBIOTIC USE IS UNNECESSARY.

FACT

IN HIS NOBEL PRIZE ACCEPTANCE SPEECH IN 1945, FLEMING GAVE A WARNING ABOUT THE FUTURE USE OF ANTIBIOTICS, PREDICTING THE PROBLEM OF ANTIBIOTIC RESISTANCE.

HOW SERIOUS IS THE PROBLEM?

Antibiotic resistance is now present in every country. Infections caused by antibiotic-resistant bacteria are much harder to treat, the results for patients are less successful and the cost is much higher. Scientists think that if nothing is done to limit our use of antibiotics or to find new classes of antibiotics, drug-resistant infections are likely to kill an extra 10 million people each year worldwide. Bacteria are showing signs of becoming resistant to so-called last-resort antibiotics – those that are used when everything else has failed. A last-resort antibiotic called colistin has shown signs of bacteria developing resistance to it. It has stayed effective over many years because it has been used very rarely due to its side effects. Farmers, however, have been using colistin to make animals grow faster and bigger. Scientists think that this is how resistance to this antibiotic began.

In some countries, including the US, around 80% of all antibiotics are given to livestock, mainly to produce extra growth in healthy animals.

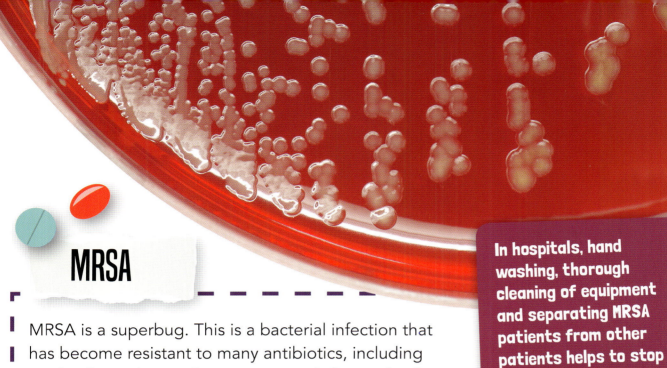

MRSA

In hospitals, hand washing, thorough cleaning of equipment and separating MRSA patients from other patients helps to stop MRSA from spreading.

MRSA is a superbug. This is a bacterial infection that has become resistant to many antibiotics, including methicillin and penicillin. MRSA stands for methicillin-resistant Staphylococcus aureus. Around 30% of people carry the Staphylococcus aureus bacterium on their skin or in their nose without it causing any problems, but if it gets inside the body, it can cause infections, including skin diseases and wound infections. Some infections, such as septicaemia (blood poisoning) can be fatal. MRSA is highly contagious and spreads easily between people, and between people and objects. It can survive for days on hospital surfaces such as door knobs, towels, curtains and plastic aprons. Although MRSA commonly affects people in hospital, increasing numbers of cases are happening outside hospitals, for example through skin-to-skin contact in sports such as rugby and in places where many people live together, such as care homes and prisons.

FACT

SCIENTISTS IN THE US HAVE FOUND TWO SUBSTANCES CALLED TAROXIN A AND B WHICH, WHEN USED WITH ANTIBIOTICS SUCH AS PENICILLIN, APPEAR TO KILL OFF MRSA, BUT MUCH RESEARCH REMAINS TO BE DONE.

ANTIBIOTICS IN THE FUTURE

The **WORLD HEALTH ORGANIZATION** (WHO) has warned that, due to the rise of resistance, the world could be approaching a time when common infections that appeared to have been wiped out by antibiotics could, once again, become fatal. It suggests that if nothing is done to deal with the problem, life-saving and life-changing procedures, such as transplants and joint replacements, could become too dangerous to carry out.

HUMAN ORGAN

Transplant surgery would be impossible without effective antibiotics.

If antibiotics become totally ineffective, it will affect everyone, not just those living in countries with lower standards of healthcare. New classes of antibiotics are urgently needed but it is very expensive and takes a long time for drug companies to attempt to discover, test and market new antibiotics. If a new antibiotic then becomes resistant quickly, the drug company may not be able to make a profit. For this reason, many drug companies are concentrating on producing drugs to fight cancer and heart disease.

In an attempt to find new classes of antibiotic, researchers have been investigating a wider range of environments. They hope that by looking at remote and hostile areas of the world, they may find organisms that produce previously undiscovered antibiotic substances. A team of British scientists has been looking at ocean environments, for example, while Canadian researchers are carrying out experiments on bacteria found deep inside caves.

CINNAMON

Cinnamon, lavender, geranium, lemongrass and thyme are natural antibiotic substances that may prove to be helpful in treating patients who have developed resistance to normal antibiotics.

UNDER OUR NOSES

Researchers have discovered a bacterium in the human nose called Staphylococcus lugdunensis. They found that the bacterium produces an antibiotic substance, which they have managed to recreate in the laboratory. Named lugdunin, it has proved effective in treating MRSA. Although MRSA is resistant to many types of antibiotic, it does not appear to develop resistance to lugdunin. Further work is needed before lugdunin can ever be used to treat humans.

BACTERIOPHAGES

Bacteriophages (say: back-TEER-ee-oh-fayges), also known as phages, are naturally-occurring viruses that are used to attack and kill bacteria. They were used in the 1920s and 1930s in Russia, but the introduction of antibiotics meant that their use reduced. Many countries are now researching phages to see if they might be helpful in the fight against antibiotic-resistant superbugs.

THIS ILLUSTRATION SHOWS OF BACTERIOPHAGES ATTACKING A BACTERIUM.

27

TREATMENTS FOR INFECTION BEFORE ANTIBIOTICS

Before the introduction of antibiotics, treatments for infections were based on traditional beliefs and customs. Some were effective, but people had no idea why. In 1676, using a primitive microscope, Dutch scientist Antonie van Leeuwenhoek was the first to see and record details of bacteria in water. The connection between these bacteria and infection, however, was not discovered until the 19th century.

LOUIS PASTEUR

PASTEUR, KOCH AND LISTER

The work of French scientist Louis Pasteur (1822–1895) and German doctor Robert Koch (1843–1910) proved germ theory – the idea that diseases are caused by the presence and action of bacteria and other microorganisms. Through a series of experiments, Pasteur showed that decay is caused by bacteria and that these bacteria can be destroyed by heating. Koch proved the idea that a particular bacterium causes a particular disease, identifying the bacteria that cause **ANTHRAX** in 1876 and tuberculosis in 1882. A British surgeon called Joseph Lister (1827–1912) wanted to stop patients who had undergone a successful operation from dying later from infection. After studying Pasteur's work, he introduced the use of carbolic acid, an antiseptic that he used to clean wounds and prevent infection.

STATUE OF JOSEPH LISTER

Before the work of Lister, who became known as 'the father of antiseptic surgery', surgeons operated without even washing their hands or equipment.

BREAD MOULD AND HONEY

Long before Fleming's discovery, many ancient civilisations, including the ancient Egyptians and Greeks, had noticed that mouldy bread wrapped around a wound prevented or healed infection. Honey has been used in wound healing since the time of an ancient civilisation called the Sumerians in 2000 B.C. Its high sugar content damages bacterial cells and stops them from growing and multiplying. It also contains an **ENZYME** called glucose oxidase that turns oxygen into a substance called hydrogen peroxide, which kills bacteria.

The most effective honey is manuka, which is derived from the flowers of tea tree, a plant that has antibacterial properties.

SILVER AND MERCURY

The ancient Egyptians, Greeks, Romans and others knew that silver containers kept water and food pure. This was very important during wars, when fresh supplies might be hard to find. An ancient civilisation called the Macedonians used silver plates to help wounds to heal. Even into the 1900s, surgeons were using silver foil for wound dressings to prevent infection. Current research is looking at ways in which silver might be used to fight bacteria that have become resistant to antibiotics.

ROMAN SILVER DRINKING CUP

QUININE

CINCHONA TREE

Quinine is a substance that has traditionally been used to treat **MALARIA**, a life-threatening disease. It is obtained from the bark of the cinchona tree in South America. The bark is dried, ground into a powder and mixed with water to make a drink. The use of cinchona bark was first described by missionaries in the 1600s, but it may have been used long before that. Quinine is still used today but it has been largely replaced with human-made drugs based on it.

CINCHONA BARK

BLOOD LETTING

Blood letting was used to treat infection for thousands of years. It was believed that the body contained four fluids – blood, phlegm (say: flem), yellow bile and blackbile – and that these must be kept in balance. Infections were thought to be caused by too much blood in the body. Blood was removed by making a cut or by placing heated glass cups onto the skin, which caused bruising. Blood-sucking worms called leeches were also used. Blood letting was often carried out by a barber, rather than a doctor.

Many barbershops displayed a pole with red and white, or red, white and blue (US) stripes above the door, to let people know that they performed blood letting. The red is said to symbolise blood, and white to symbolise bandages.